W9-AAW-319

24 Christmas Stories for Little Ones

Cover illustration : Gretchen VonS
Layout Design : Élisabeth Hebert, assisted by Amélie Hosteing
Layout : Sophie Boscardin and Gilles Malgonne

24 Christmas Stories for Little Ones

Ignatius

Magnificat®

Contents

December 1

The Advent Calendar

Lewis received an Advent calendar this evening. But . . . there is nothing to see except an empty path leading to closed stable doors. Lewis is a little disappointed.

"Well, why don't you try looking for window number 1?" his mommy asks with a smile.

Lewis' eyes light up with curiosity. There it is! And when he opens the first window, Lewis finds a person walking along the path. He is carrying a lantern, the first light in the dark night of the calendar!

Then Daddy says, "With this nice little man, we've set off on the road toward Jesus. We're going to prepare our hearts for Christmas."

"But how?" asks Lewis.
Mommy thinks
for a moment:
"By spreading smiles
around us, like little lamps
to light the way.

Jesus, I want to walk
toward you.
Help me to spread joy
all around me!

"They'll lead us to
the doors of the stable
where the greatest
Light of all awaits us!"

December 2

A Wreath for the Long Wait till Christmas

It is cold in the little monastery of Bergen in Sweden. The monks are running out of wood for heating and have very few candles left for light. And now that snow is piling up on the roads, there won't be any more logs coming.

In fact, there are still four candles left, but the monks are saving them to mark the four weeks until Christmas on the Advent wreath.

On the first Sunday of Advent, the abbot lights the first candle. The monks draw near. The candle warms them with its soft glow.

And so, each Sunday, the monks gather around the Advent wreath for their weekly ration of warmth and light.

When at last, on Christmas night, the final candle goes out . . . someone knocks at the door of the abbey. There stands a man with an armful of logs and four candles. Jesus is born! The Light of the world!

Christmas
is still far away.
Teach us to be
patient, Lord,
and to prepare
our hearts well.

December 3

The Annunciation

This is the story of what happened in Nazareth a little over two thousand years ago.

Mary lives in the village of Nazareth. She is engaged to Joseph, the carpenter. One day, God sends the angel Gabriel with great news to announce to her.

Gabriel enters Mary's house and says: "Hail, Mary, the Lord is with you. You will soon be expecting a baby, a little boy whom you will name Jesus. He will be the Son of God."

Mary cannot understand: "But how can that be? I'm not even married to Joseph yet!"

The angel reassures her: “Mary, nothing is impossible for God!”

Mary trusts in God. So she says to Gabriel: “I am the servant of the Lord. Yes—I am ready for everything you have said!”

Mary,
sometimes I say No
when Mommy asks me
to do something.
Help me to say Yes,
like you.

December 4

Great Things Grow from Little Seeds

Snowflakes the size of golf balls are falling, and the twins have their noses stuck to the window: snow is so rare in Southern California.

Suddenly, Grandma calls them: “Emily, Maggie, come look! Three huge snowflakes have fallen into three little bowls!”

Of course, Grandma is just joking: they are really three cotton balls that she has sprinkled with water.

"Here, girls, take these beans and plant them in the cotton."

"Why?" asks Emily.

"Because it's a tradition on December 4th! These seeds will be growing until Christmas, when we'll offer the first sprouts to Jesus."

Dear God, thank you
for my family.
Thank you for the happiness
you give me day after day.

"Does he like beans?" Maggie asks in astonishment.

Grandma smiles: "It's said that the growing shoots are a sign of the New Life God is giving us through Jesus."

December 5

The Visitation

Mary of Nazareth is on a journey. A few days ago, the angel Gabriel told her that her cousin Elizabeth is also expecting a baby. So right away, she decides to hurry off to visit her. And here she is, on her way, seated on a donkey.

After a long trip, Mary arrives at Elizabeth's house. She goes in and greets her cousin.

Elizabeth cries, "How happy I am to see you! And my baby is, too! He just jumped for joy inside me. It's as though he guessed you are carrying a treasure. I am so happy to welcome you, dear cousin.

"You are most blessed among all women, and blessed, too, is your baby. Mary, you will be the Mother of my Lord!"

"Yes," replies Mary, "God has done great things for me!"

Dear God,
I, too, want to dance
and jump for joy!
You do wonders,
and you love us
so much!

December 6

Saint Nicholas

It is Saint Nicholas' special day today! In Germany, as in many countries all over the world, children are hoping that he will come to visit them, bringing special gifts ...

Kristian already has his velvet stocking hanging next to the fireplace. He looks at it for a long time and then asks his mother: "Who exactly is Saint Nicholas?"

Mom cannot help smiling: "Saint Nicholas lived a long time ago. He was such a kind and generous bishop, he gave all he possessed to the poor; and he spent his life helping people around him. But he was also very humble, and he did all his gift-giving secretly! Saint Nicholas is an example for all of us! And I'm sure he has been the model for lots of gift-givers!"

"Mom, I want to make my own secret gift, too!" Kristian says with excitement. "To Anke, down the street … she is so sad since her Dad got sick! If I go hang my stocking on her door tonight, Saint Nicholas could bring her candy canes!"

O good Saint Nicholas,
patron saint
of little children,
help us to be generous
of heart.

December 7

Two Little Pine Trees

There was a famine that year in the country. Sean hears his parents sigh, "Soon it will be Christmas, and we have nothing left to eat . . ."

Terribly worried, the little boy thinks to himself, "I must earn some money!"

Sean has an idea: he goes to the forest to find pines to sell as Christmas trees. But he is little and only manages to uproot two scrawny little ones.

In the marketplace, no one even stops to look at them.

When it is evening, a gardener takes pity on the little boy shivering in the cold. "I'll buy your trees, a golden coin apiece."

And so, having saved Sean's family, the gardener goes home and plants the pine trees, thinking, "They're so weak, they'll surely die."

But, on Christmas Day, what a big surprise for the gardener when he arrives home from Mass!

Jesus, help me
to be generous,
and please bring joy
to everyone.

The two little pines have grown into two enormous trees, now bursting with health!

December 8

The Christmas Nativity Scene

Just as they do every year in December, Benjamin and Emily are helping their parents set up the Nativity scene at home. Mom and Dad have brought out the box where all the figurines are kept wrapped up nice and tight in tissue paper. Dad puts together the stable; the two children lay out a path with pebbles; and Mom hangs pretty stars above it.

Then, very carefully, each of them chooses a figurine.
“Where shall we put this shepherd?” asks Emily.
“And the baker with her basket?” asks Mom.
“Oh, that’s the one I made!” exclaims Benjamin.

And there it is:
the Nativity scene is
almost complete!

On Christmas Day, Benjamin and Emily will get out the last figurine and place him tenderly in the middle of all his friends. And then they will all sing to him:

December 9

The Three Little Trees

On a hillside in a forest near Jerusalem, three little trees dream of greatness.

"When I grow up, I'd like to become a treasure chest", says the first.

"And I'll be a great big ship voyaging the seven seas."

"And as for me, I'll be so tall, the whole world will look up to me!"

But nothing turns out quite as expected . . .

The first tree was made into a manger.

Yet, one night, a mommy laid her baby in it. His name was Jesus, the Son of God. So, the dream of the first tree really did come true: there it was, bearing a treasure more precious than any other.

The second tree became a simple little fishing boat.

But one day, Jesus, now a man, got into the boat to speak to the crowd. It is true, the boat did not travel far, but the words Jesus spoke were more beautiful than anything the tree had ever heard—and that was worth all the voyages in the world.

The last tree was cut into simple beams of wood.

Nevertheless, one day, those beams were set up on the top of a hill in the shape of a cross for that same man named Jesus. The tree was so saddened by this terrible torture.

But then it realized what an amazing sign of love the cross was. From then on, people would look up to it with their hearts full of hope.

Lord, you are
the treasure of my heart.
I want to prepare my heart
to welcome you.

December 10

The Magi

Three men are crossing the desert guided by a bright star.

One morning, a bandit stops them on the road: "What are you carrying in these chests?"

"Gold, incense, and myrrh", the travelers answer.

"Hand over all your merchandise!"

“But, we’re not merchants; we’re Magi! The star that guides us heralds the birth of a child who will change the world. These gifts are for him.”

The bandit backs away—he could not steal things from a baby like that!

“Then, I’m going to follow this star, too.”

“Would you like to travel along with us?”

“No, first I too must go prepare a gift for the child.”

As the bandit gallops off into the distance, the Magi continue their journey at the slow pace of their camels.

"This baby has already begun to change the world!" murmurs the eldest.

Jesus,
I pray to you
for Christians
all over the world
who are preparing
for Christmas
just as I am doing.

December 11

Christmas beyond Borders

Alex and Lang-hao both have the same school project for Christmas. Alex lives in America, and Lang-hao lives on the other side of the world in China. But each of them has to choose one of his toys to offer as a gift to the other.

Alex sorts through his toys. Too worn out! Too dopey! Too small! It is so hard to choose . . .

Unless he gives him his fire engine! But that one is his favorite.

Lang-hao looks at his toys: his yo-yo that lights up, his dragon marionette, and the tambourine with ribbons that he loves so much. Could he really agree to give that away?

On Christmas night, Alex unwraps Lang-hao's tambourine. It is so beautiful, he forgets all about his fire engine!!

On the other side of the world, Lang-hao cannot believe his eyes: a fire engine just like the one he has always dreamed of!

"Merry Christmas, Lang-hao", thinks Alex.

"*Sheng dan kuai le*",* whispers Lang-hao.

* "Merry Christmas" in Chinese.

December 12

Christmas Card Greetings

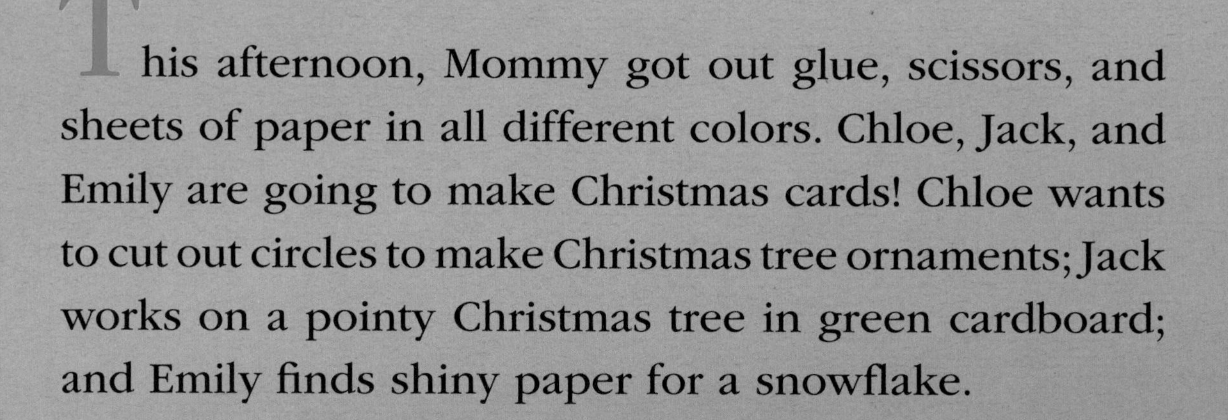

This afternoon, Mommy got out glue, scissors, and sheets of paper in all different colors. Chloe, Jack, and Emily are going to make Christmas cards! Chloe wants to cut out circles to make Christmas tree ornaments; Jack works on a pointy Christmas tree in green cardboard; and Emily finds shiny paper for a snowflake.

“And to whom shall we send these beautiful cards?” Mommy asks.

“One for Grandpa and Grandma, one for Godfather, one for Auntie . . .”, Chloe answers.

“I want to send some, too!” says Emily.

“I’ve got an idea”, says Jack. “How about if we think of someone we really appreciate in the neighborhood?”

Lord, I entrust to
your care all those I love
and appreciate.
For each of them,
I send smiles and laughter
along with my card.

"Yes! I choose the school crossing guard."

"And I choose the mailman."

"And I choose the nice men who collect the garbage because, without them, what a mess it would be—our street really wouldn't be a pretty sight!"

December 13

Peace on Earth!

After school, Paul and Lucy are annoyed with each other. And soon enough, an argument breaks out. Hearing loud sobs, Mom comes running: “What on earth is going on?” Lucy shows her the Christmas star she made in class. Paul has torn it up!

Mom comforts Lucy and patches together the pretty golden paper as best as she can.

Paul is not very proud of himself. He goes searching through his schoolbag. "Uh . . . Lucy, I have a present for you. I made it this afternoon."

He holds out a brightly decorated candle holder to his sister.

"I was thinking of you as I was making it. Because today is Saint Lucy's Day, the feast of light."

Tears and anger are forgotten! Lucy hugs her brother.

That evening, Paul's candle holder will grace the dinner table as a reminder that Christmas is coming, the great feast day of peace.

Jesus, in the Bible
you are called the "Prince of Peace".
Help me to make peace
around me, with my
brothers, my sisters,
and my friends.

December 14

A Christmas Tree for Baby Jesus

It was God who made the earth, the flowers, the trees, and all the animals. And it was he who made the little fir tree, too. So when the little fir tree heard that Jesus was about to be born, it wanted to give him the best welcome it could to thank God for this wonderful gift. And so it stood up tall and proud.

Soon the snow fell and covered its branches. Birds of all colors came to perch on it. And a star even came to sit right on top of it. How beautiful the little fir tree looked!

When people saw it, they thought there was no better way to give glory to the Son of God. So they all put up little fir trees in their own homes.

Thank you,
Lord, for the beauty
of your creation.
Thank you for the snow
and the fir trees
and the stars.

And ever since then, at Christmas, people still decorate a Christmas tree in memory of that first one that wanted to honor Jesus.

December 15

Little Hans' Wooden Shoes

In a little town in the Netherlands, all the children come bursting out of midnight Mass. They rush home to place their shoes near the Christmas cradle—just as other children elsewhere hang up their stockings. Tomorrow morning, they will find them full of a thousand and one little gifts and goodies. Only Hans, the little orphan, is in no hurry. He knows he will not find anything in his shoes.

Hans walks slowly back to the orphanage. On the way, he notices a little child asleep on a drafty porch.

"Poor little thing", thinks Hans, as he spots the child's bare foot sticking out. Without a second thought, he pulls off one of his wooden shoes and slips it on the child's foot before he goes hobbling off.

The next morning, Hans wakes to discover a miracle: his one remaining wooden shoe has been filled with gifts.

In the Christmas manger, Jesus is cuddling a wooden shoe given to him by a little boy. Because he was the slumbering child Hans had seen that night!

Jesus, I would like
to give you a present.
I would like to offer you my heart
and to please you always.

December 16

A Good Deed for Christmas

Gideon is a bit of a mischievous boy.

He leaves his things scattered all over the house—his pants in the living room; his towel and his soap in the kitchen; and his schoolbag and toy planes in the bathroom!

“We have got to sort this out!” says Mom. “Soon it will be Christmas. In one week Uncle George will arrive with your cousin Simon. Wouldn’t you rather decorate the house with these?”

And Mom shows him beautiful garlands and strings of light, Christmas tree ornaments, and Nativity figurines.

Gideon thinks about it: "It would be fun to have the house look pretty for Christmas!"

So he makes up his mind what to do. He gathers up all his toys and puts them in a box.

Look, Jesus,
how beautiful my house is.
And I will make my heart
just as beautiful
to welcome you!

He hangs up his clothes in the closet and returns the soap and towel to the bathroom.

Well done! Now everything is ready to welcome Uncle George and cousin Simon!

December 17

Christmas in Poland

It is the night before Christmas. Piotr has not put on the light in his bedroom. Standing in the dark, he seems to be waiting for a signal at the window . . .

"There it is! The first star!" he cries at last.

"It's time for dinner, then!" says his mom.

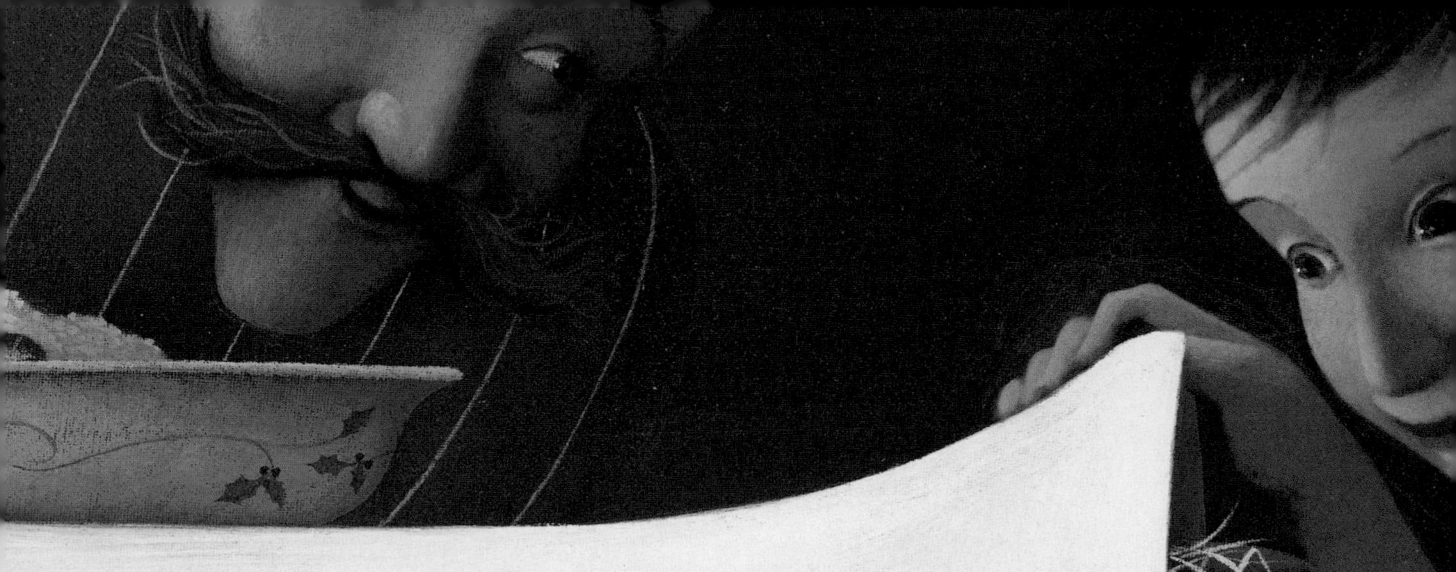

Piotr is at the table in the twinkling of an eye. He peeks under the white tablecloth: Perfect! Daddy has laid bits of straw underneath in memory of the stable where Jesus was born.

"But there's one place setting too many!"

"As always on Christmas night", Mom reminds him. "That's Jesus' place."

In the meantime, Dad is about to cut everyone a piece of optalek, a thin wafer decorated on both sides with the Nativity scene.

"Wait, I want to look at it first!"

"You're right. We only see it once a year. Let's make the most of it!"

*Jesus, bless all
the families of the world,
and be near to those who
have no family with whom
to celebrate Christmas.*

"Wesolych Swiat!" cries Mom with joy, which, in Polish, means quite simply "Merry Christmas!"

December 18

The Donkey in the Christmas Stable

"My coat is gray, and people say I'm stubborn. I've got long ears, and I refuse to budge if I don't feel like it. I carry very heavy loads, and people, too. Who am I . . . ?

“. . . I’m the donkey in the Christmas stable.

“Don’t listen to people who say I’m dumb. Because I understand lots of things . . . I traveled the road from Nazareth all the way here, carrying Mary on my back. She’s expecting a baby, you know!”

"During that long trip, she told me something extraordinary was about to happen on earth. Have you heard? Me, I just wait patiently.

Tonight, in my house,
I'm happy.
Thank you, my God,
for all you have given me.

"But if soon there's a little baby who needs warming up, I'm ready.

"Here in this stable in Bethlehem, I'm the happiest donkey on earth."

December 19

Treats from Provence

Mrs. Agosti has thirteen children.

Phew! What work, thirteen children! And yet, Mrs. Agosti always has time for each one of them, whether it's time for cuddles and kisses or, before Christmas, for baking!

With one of the children, she makes light, sweet buns. They laugh because they get flour on their noses. With another, she makes crispy “beggarman” pastries, in honor of the monks who beg for alms for the poor.

“Mmmm! Yummy!” they cry, gleefully dipping their fingers in the dough.

With the littlest one, she arranges a basket of fruit.

“Everyone will think it’s very beautiful”, they say, clapping their hands as they admire their work.

On the night before Christmas, each child carries his plate of treats to the table. That is why, according to the French tradition in the southern region of Provence, the Agosti family enjoys thirteen desserts, each as special as the one who made it.

Jesus, we await you so eagerly
and with such happiness.
Thank you for the joy of our Christmas
preparations.

December 20

The Angels' Christmas Preparations

The day Mary agreed to become the mother of Jesus, the angels held a meeting in heaven:

"We have nine months to prepare for the birth!"

"We have to wait nine months until Christmas?!"

"We'll need all that time to work on our music." The angels compose such melodious songs that the stars in the sky applaud their rehearsals. At last, the great night arrives.

"Who would like to announce the birth of my Son to mankind?" asks God.

No one raises his hand, because the angels are so good, none of them wants to outshine the others!

God smiles: "Okay. You will all go together to bend over the earth."

The joyful crowd of angels gathers together above Bethlehem. They all brandish their instruments and clear their throats.

The orchestra conductor strikes up the music with a flap of his wings, and the Christmas concert begins!

Dear Lord, it seems such a long time to wait until Christmas! Help me to prepare myself to make it a truly beautiful celebration!

December 21

The Christmas Guest

Peter and Madeleine have a neighbor called Mrs. Oddy. The twins are afraid of her because she is a little hunchbacked, always wears the same old gray coat, and never says very much.

And now Daddy has had the strange idea of inviting her for Christmas Day.

“It’s sad to be all alone for Christmas, and Mrs. Oddy doesn’t have any family to visit her. So, she’ll come spend a little time with us.”

On Christmas Day, Mrs. Oddy arrives with a little present for everyone.

Over dinner, she tells amazing stories about things that happened a long time ago when she was still a little girl.

In fact, Mrs. Oddy isn't odd at all. And under that old gray coat of hers, she has a heart of gold.

Lord,
let me have a smile
for people who
are all alone,
so they won't feel
so sad.

December 22

The Shepherds

"Wake up, little Tony! Wake up! Do you hear that music?" the grandfather shepherd asks his little grandson. "Do you see that great light?"

Little Tony sits up, and even the little lambs stand up in wonder, thinking they have heard the voice of their master. The stars seem to be lighting up the sky so brightly! Songs are coming from everywhere! Suddenly, Tony points toward the sky: "Look! A new star! There, right above us!"

The old shepherd nods: "Yes, it's a new star, Tony . . . something extraordinary is happening." And he goes on: "An angel of God has spoken to us. He said a little child has been born this night in Bethlehem. He's the Savior of the whole world!"

"Can we go see him, Grandpa?"

But the old shepherd has already set off, his heart full of joy at the thought of seeing their Savior. "Come on, Tony! We must hurry!"

Jesus,
even if it is very
cold outside,
my heart is warm
with love for you.

December 23

Herod and the Three Wise Kings

It is night when the three wise men arrive at the palace of Herod.

They are tired and covered in dust. But you can still tell from their rich clothing that they are important people.

"We are following a new star", they explain to Herod. "It announces the birth of a king."

"A rival!" Herod thinks nastily to himself.

"A Savior", say the smiling Magi, with hope in their eyes. "Do you know where we can find him?"

The scholars of the palace are definite: the child is to be found in Bethlehem.

"Go and find this king", says Herod. "Then come tell me where he is, so that I, too, can go worship him."

The Magi set off again on the road.

Herod awaits their return with hatred in his heart. But days go by, and no one arrives. The Magi have taken a different route home to protect the Son of God from the anger of this wicked king.

Thank you, Jesus, for coming at Christmas for all men on earth, those from the north and the south, those from the east and the west.

December 24

Christmas Night

It is cold, and the shepherds sleeping in the hills around Bethlehem shiver in the winter wind.

Suddenly, they tremble with fear as well: an angel has just appeared before them!

"Do not be afraid", the angel says to them. "I come to bring you great news: a Savior has just been born in a stable in Bethlehem."

The shepherds run and quickly find the baby of whom the angel spoke.

"There was no place in the inn", Joseph explains to them. "So we took shelter here just in time for the birth."

The mother, Mary, watches over the Baby Jesus with wonder.

Overwhelmed with joy, the shepherds bow down before him.

Then they set off running through the streets of Bethlehem, crying out to the people: "Wake up! Come quickly to see the Son of God!"

For how could they keep this wonderful news to themselves?

Thank you,
dear God,
for giving men the most
beautiful gift in the world:
the birth of Jesus.
Thank you for the joy of
Christmas!

Original French edition:
24 Histoires de Noël pour attendre Jésus

ISBN Ignatius Press 978-1-58617-682-2. • ISBN Magnificat 978-1-936260-33-1

Printed by Tien Wah Press, Malaysia
Printed on September, 2013
Job Number MGN 13016-02
Printed in Malaysia in compliance with the Consumer Protection Safety Act, 2008.